THE #1 THING WRONG WITH THE BIBLE

UNCOMMON WISDOM FOR HEALING YOUR CHURCH HURT

LONNA HARDIN

SONGBIRD PUBLISHING

FIRST THINGS FIRST

HAVE you met someone on your spiritual journey that turned you off the path to deepen your faith? Or have you had a bad experience with a church leader or member vowing never to return?

Did you grow up in church striving to be perfect? Do you see the world as black, white, good, or bad? Do you feel you've lost your way?

Have you become a Pharisee or Sadducee overdosing on religion? Do you swallow a camel and strain at a gnat? Do you believe heaven is only for a select few and hell is a place created to punish sinners?

Do you believe people fall into two major categories? Sinner or saint. Did someone make you feel there's no place for you in the Kingdom of God? No, you say?

Are you a beautiful woman who spent Sundays searching for your Boaz only to find yourself a side chick? Somehow you found yourself swept off your feet by a married man? Are you ashamed of what you'd become?

Did you decide to settle for seconds believing having a piece of a man was better than none at all? Are you the woman that took the late-night playing phone sex operator to someone who needed a few more amens?

Did you believe all was well if the lights were off and no one could see?

You could even be a struggling caregiver who looked for help from your local church only to find none? Did you pray to ask God to send someone to check on you to make sure you were mentally intact? Whatever the reason you picked up this book, here's the good news. You're in good company!

If you are apart of the institution called the physical church the church bug has bitten you. Expectations, high optimism, simultaneous disappointment, and brokenhearted traitors may have let you down. You may have endured a walk so hurtful, devastating, and mind-blowing you wanted to run away. Let's talk.

We all tend to merge God, the bible, His people, and the church.

Have you debated walking away from it all? Did you turn your back on God and the church? If so, grab a chair, some coffee, and take notes. This book is for you.

Let me introduce myself. I 'm the church usher, praise team leader, or intercessor. I'm the everyday deacon, trustee, church administrator, secretary, youth pastor, and more. You recognize me, don't you?

I'm the exhausted clergyman, the saint in the pew, and choir member. Do you know the one who comes to church Sunday after Sunday? I am the person looking for more of God. I pray someone will tell me my purpose and lead me in the path I should go. You have more than likely never noticed me, let me tell you more about who I am. I come to church week after week. If I listen to enough sermons, I'll finally build enough faith to move and take action. I take God at His word. If I pray long enough, fast, serve, and give my all, I'll get it all back in return.

Where is the church when I need it most? Isn't this what serving God is all about? Is reading my bible, walking by faith, and living by the scriptures all in vain? "What's wrong with the church?" "What's wrong with the bible?" "What's wrong with God's people?" Great question.

I'm going to let you in on one of the best-kept secrets of our time. It's something religion doesn't want you to know. I'll share the number one thing wrong with the bible. You see I too asked those same hard questions. Met with tough days of introspection and reflection. My grandparents went to church. My father and mother went to church. My ancestors went to church.

After spending my life in the church, I often asked, "Is this all life is about? Is being a Christian another catchphrase worn by a social club for weekends only? Is it a place to go jump, shout, sing, and feel good? Does everyone transform into a different person when they get home? What is all the fuss about?

I was born into a Christian family. The daughter of a preacher, a man who revered and respected everywhere he went. He could preach sermons without any notes. He had a way with words and women. My father was charming, intelligent, wise, and magnetic. He gave himself to a life of service. When he died in 2017 at the age of 88, he'd founded three churches. All still exist today.

I wasn't raised by my father. When I was born, my father and mother divorced. I grew up with a stigma never knowing my true full identity. I searched for it all my life. I searched in people, relationships, extracurricular activities, and attempted to fit in. I didn't know our rich legacy until my father passed.

After he died, children, he'd baptized as babies reached out on social channels. Each had become Pastors. I heard story after story of his impact. Until then, I never understood his heart and reach.

With this knowledge and the weight of walking in my father's footsteps, I write this book. I also write with urgency and purpose. I carry an even heavier burden of our Heavenly Father's heart. Many of us lack knowing our own identities in Him and the richness of our full inheritance in Christ. This is a vital message for those called to be His.

I grew up needing the affirmation of a father. I searched for it looking to fill the void. So many of us long for affirmation. We come to church. We give our lives to God. We join a local church looking for a family of believers.

We want someone to embrace us, take us by the hand, and lead us closer to the light. Oftentimes, we come from broken, traumatic families. We may not understand our place, role, or how to navigate this new territory.

This lack of understanding can govern our relationships. It can lead us back into the same self-sabotaging patterns we leave behind. When you picked up this book, did you think it would be an opportunity to bash the people of God? Did you think it was a tell-all?

Did you think this book would allow you to vent to someone who understands? The answer is both yes and no. Yes, because in all my searching for a deeper walk with God, I too looked for answers. I experienced the brokenness, rejection, abandonment, and abuse, and in the church.

At times I felt held down, forced to hold still and robbed of my voice. I felt depleted of my greatest gifting, time, and calling. I felt the precious things I held close to my heart were gone.

Whatever you've experienced or been through, know this. Your personality, who you are, and what you have to offer is enough. Many have abandoned the path toward God, looking for approval and needing affirmation. It's the number one thing wrong with the church. It's also the #1 thing wrong with the bible.

WHAT'S GOING ON?

UNTIL A FEW YEARS AGO, I was like thousands of others. I retired and withdrew my church membership. Hurt rejected and feeling betrayed, I refused to join another church. I'd had enough.

I'd left my former church 15 years ago. Bad experiences left me broken, confused and feeling lonelier than ever. Let me be clear about one thing. Like many reading right now, I didn't leave God. I left church people.

Tired, I'd had enough of the lying, two-faced backbiting. I was over the respect of persons. The snobbery was way more than I could handle. The constant character assassinations and robbery were too much to bear.

I refused to belittled. The condescending, belittling undertones made me want to run and hide. There was a lack of mutual respect missing that made me angry and defiant. The culture required I act as if I didn't see it. No longer would I be numb to the trauma felt by the "least of these."

I wanted the cycle to end. It seemed to control and witchcraft on display Sunday after Sunday. They each wore a suit and tie, some hiding behind titles. Sorcery and divination hiding in the pews unchecked and unmasked.

Money appeared to become the primary focus. Accountability to God's word seemed obsolete. No one was talking about it. It felt ridiculous. Hypersexuality was also out of hand. My thoughts, "If the church is like the world, why do I need it? Is this what I've given my life for?" Guess what saints? You can have it!"

This stance didn't happen overnight. It wasn't one church, Pastor, member, or thing. I was rebelling against the entire system. I didn't quite understand why. I blamed brother or sister so and so for my hurt, anger, and pain. My finger pointed every step of the way.

At that point, I ran. I ran from the church. The more I ran, the more I realized it wasn't about the church at all. It was about me. My confidence and trust misplaced, I'd put it in man. The bible tells us to put no confidence in the flesh, but it's exactly what I'd done. Deceived, I believed the church or system began from the outside in, instead of the inside out.

Jeremiah 17:9 KJV

"The heart is desperately wicked and deceitful above all things, who can know it. I the Lord try the heart and reins to give every man according to his heart and the fruit of his doing."

My confidence no longer was in God alone. It was in systems, structures, and ideologies. I stopped filtering life and the church through the word of God. As I ran deeper away from the church, I ran deeper away from who I was.

I became more withdrawn. Ashamed and embarrassed, personal failures, shortcomings, and character flaws dominated my view. I didn't want to associate with the calling and house of God.

I had experienced church hurt before. First, in my teens after serving the church for years. Second, during my young adulthood. This time had a different sting. A young high school girl trying to fit in but standing out like a sore thumb.

As a child, God would show me things. I was clueless about why. I would know things without knowing how I knew. I was preacher without every trying to preach. Words came from the mouth with conviction and power. People said things like, "You think you know everything." I'd disrupt situations and circumstances without any intent.

Always a black sheep, I didn't talk or think like everyone else. Always surrounded by many friends, but never being able to associate with a group or clique. I knew how to be friends with everyone. My goal was to stay under the radar and go along with the crowd. It never worked.

Time and time again, I had very deep experiences with God. As I grew older, I gave my life to God. Over time, I began to submit. As I did, these experiences grew stronger. I'd see dreams and visions at a young age.

I remember the first vision at 13. I broke the news to my mom. My stepfather was having an affair. We were at a home bible study. I saw a triangle on the ground. I couldn't make it out. I kept tracing it with my foot. As I started to speak what I saw, I saw My mom, stepfather, and a third woman. God revealed it. When she confronted him about it, it was true.

I remember a dream I also had around 13. We lived in Texas at the time. I dreamed of my Aunt who lived in Michigan. I felt an urgency I can't describe. I awoke from the dream and told my mom. She called my aunt that morning. They talked for hours. Shortly after, my aunt died.

At 19, the same thing happened. It dreamed of my best friend I hadn't seen since 16. In it, I saw a stage. Her life was flashing before my eyes in pictures. Disturbed and shaken, I again told my mom. She responded, "Pray."

I said a short prayer and called my friend. I thought nothing more about it. Years later, my younger sister visited Texas. It was then I found out, Taseanya had died. It was after I'd had the dream. My sister returned home to a funeral program. It was full of her life in pictures.

God's hand was always in my life. He spoke to me in the most peculiar ways. I never saw myself as special or somehow possessing a power no one else possessed. Whether I was in the church or not, God always found a way to reveal himself or his plan.

I'll never forget another dream. I'd met this young man in 1999. Ten years later, I saw him in the strangest dream. Shaken, I awoke and went to find him on Facebook. I wanted to check on him. I told him about the awkward dream. I saw him hiding in the corner naked. After our messenger chat, he shared he was believing God for healing from HIV Aids.

On my journey with God, so many unique things happened. One Sunday morning, I recall singing on my church praise team. My eyes focused on a friend standing in the back of our 500-seat church. As I was singing, I started weeping. Something in me felt the need to comfort her.

I made my way out of the pulpit walking down the stairs. When I finally got to the back of the church, I grabbed and hugged her. I couldn't stop sobbing. I bawled like a baby with no clue why. I felt the strongest sense of compassion. I needed to offer solace.

She looked at me like, "What the heck?" Within two days, her stepfather died. I'd been somewhat close to the family. After relocating, I stayed at their house for a short time. Her stepfather was a great guy. I hadn't seen him in seven years.

These things happened all my life. I never understood it. After my second church hurt experience, I wanted it all to go away. I needed to pick up the pieces and start again. I felt like the prodigal son on steroids. I couldn't run from my calling if I tried.

So, Lonna, you ask. "All that's great. I still don't get it. What is the #1 thing wrong with the bible?" I'm glad you asked.

THE ANSWER IS IN Y-O-U

YOU AND I ARE THE **#1 thing wrong with the bible.**

You heard me right. You are. You're the #1 thing wrong with the bible. Your story is missing. Stay with me. I'm 100% confident this is for you.

I've written several books. I get stopped by people asking how to tell their story all the time. approached by those who want to tell their story. They're inspired, but it never gets done.

Last year, I offered a discounted author's writing and publishing course. I felt the burden many carried with having something to share but being unable to. They didn't know how or where to begin.

Putting myself in their shoes, I remember how hard it was to get started. I had very little help. Most companies charge astronomical fees.

One day, I heard God say, "Write a book called the #1 thing that is wrong with the bible." At the time, I was very apprehensive. I vacillated on speaking out about issues I felt in my heart or holding back versus how others saw me. Although I didn't have the reach or followers, I knew I was born to help people.

This message was for the church." God began to unveil areas of growth for the church. the constant misapplication of His word. Here's what's wrong with the bible:

1. The bible is still being written. It is a living, breathing document.

2. As human beings, we fail to practice or live what we preach.

3. We give the devil too much press.

4. Many are not walking in their calling and purpose. They're waiting on you.

Let's look at each in more detail.

The Bible is a living, breathing document.

We're still writing the bible. It's created as a living, breathing document. People believe the bible ends with the book of Revelation. They think that's where it stops. Revelations are just that... a revelation.

The book of Revelation unveils Christ and the church. It does not end the word of God. It only reveals it. We're supposed to walk, live, and breathe this revelation. God's word is "line upon line and precept upon precept." We must apply it to our hearts and lives.

When Jesus came to the earth, he came standing on the word of God. He was echoing everything God said. He always said, "He did not come of himself." He came walking and talking the word. He also came quoting the prophets.

Even though Jesus came to earth as the revealed Son of God, he came as a man. Christ didn't come as a new version of Adam, he was an extension. Jesus Christ was Man 2.0.

Why is this important? It explains Christ's entire life. He lived his life around the law and on the word of the prophets. He walked on a foundation already laid. Christ came to build the house as a carpenter. He had to put a frame around it. When Jesus showed up on the scene, the word was alive, living, and still in action.

What if Jesus looked at the bible as being only past tense? What if Christ only based his relationship with God on what the prophets had written? Where would the church be? Could grace and salvation still have kicked in?

Let's review **Luke 4:18-22** to further illuminate what God is releasing in this season. The written acts and word of God were never supposed to end. Jesus goes to the synagogue. As someone gives him the book of the prophet Esaias, he opens it and reads:

Luke 4:18-22 KJV

"The Spirit of the Lord is upon me because he hath anointed me to preach the gospel to the poor; he hath sent me to heal the broken-hearted, to preach deliverance to the captives, and recovering of sight to the blind, to set at liberty them that are bruised,

To preach the acceptable year of the Lord.

And he closed the book, and he gave it again to the minister and sat down. And the eyes of all them that were in the synagogue fasted on him.

And he began to say unto them, This day is this scripture fulfilled in your ears.

And all bare him witness and wondered at the gracious words which proceeded out of his mouth. And they said, Isn't this Joseph's son?"

This scripture highlights my point. God is still raising modern-day prophets. Today's leaders must stand ready. They must take the Body of Christ to another level of dominion and maturity. We can't shrink back, hide, and refuse to stand up to the call.

As Paul said, "I'm chief among sinners." Like Paul, I can never boast of my greatness or position. Paul had been on both sides of the aisle. I too have been on both sides.

Before Paul's conversion, he persecuted and killed Christians. His past qualified him. Likewise, my past justifies, qualifies, and commissions me to carry this message.

I relate to many. I struggled through so much trying to be perfect. I hid. I acted like I had it all together. Those who knew me knew I'd been through hell and back. When I gave my life back to the Lord, he changed my soul and heart.

People would see me and say, "You look so unscathed." At the time, I didn't even know what that meant. I've been through the fire and not been burnt. Many of you also have been through. You wept with tears and pain.

Like me, you may be unsure of how God can get the glory. He alone can reconcile your story. Through every tear, embarrassment, shame, and disappointment, He's right there.

In Psalms 139:8, King David says it this way:

"If I ascend into heaven, thou art there: if I make my bed in hell, behold, thou are there.

If I take the wings of the morning and dwell in the uttermost parts of the sea:

Even there shall thy hand lead me, and thy right hand shall hold me.

If I say, Surely the darkness shall cover me: even the night shall be light about me.

Yeah, the darkness hideth not from thee: but the night shineth as the day: the darkness and the light are both alike to thee."

It's time to own your true identity. No more shame. It's time to tell your full story. People need to read more than the introduction. They can't skip through chapters two and three and go right to the end. Others must know how we fight our battles and win victories. Why do we mask the unique parts of our story that make us who we are? I talk about this in my book, "Voiceprint."

You can't hide the true parts of your voiceprint, that makes you, you. Every writer or person in the bible knew the importance of capturing the full story. Can you name one prophet, king, or leader who had overnight success?

Imagine if Jesus were on the scene now. What if he only captured selfies, "Living his best life?" Where would we be as believers? Stuck, broken, and without hope. What if Jesus only took a snapshot of His life after his time in the wilderness and resurrection?

Where would we be? Lost, still in sin, in chains and bondage. We walk free because he walked free. We breakthrough because he broke through. We are free from bondage.

Jesus took a trip to hell. He hung out on our behalf so he'd know how it feels. Then he said, "Death, you can't hold me or anyone I'm connected to!" How's that for someone who tells the entire story?

Jesus continued the story of the prophets by fulfilling them as he taught and preached. He aw himself and his life in the words of each book. The old testament was written before Jesus came into the earth. The new testament after. How many testaments would be written if every believer followed suit?

Jesus did so many works while he was alive. In **St. John 21:25** it says:

"And there are also many other things which Jesus did, the which, if they should be written every one, I suppose that even the world itself could not contain the books that should be written. Amen."

Jesus was the walking, talking, living word of God. So are you! If God never does another thing for you, you're equipped with everything you need:

Hebrews 4:12 KJV

"For the word of God is quick, and powerful, and sharper than any two-edged sword, piercing even to the dividing asunder of soul and spirit, and the joints and marrow, and is a discerner of the thoughts and intents of the heart.

Neither is there any creature that is not manifest in his sight: but all things are naked and opened unto the eyes of him with whom we have to do."

You are quick. You are powerful. You are sharper than any two-edged sword.

The word of God in you, through you, for you, by you, on you, and around you pierce. It divides asunder the soul, spirit, joints, and marrow. It's a discerner of the thoughts and intentions of the heart.

Jesus experienced what we experienced so he could testify to and for us. He's seated as a witness in heaven. He bears witness to the journey triumphing because he made it. Your life must testify too!

We as believers are "Living Epistles.

We will see tremendous growth in the Body of Christ when everyone starts sharing their testimony! Let's review this more.

We're the living word. We're are living stories written on the earth. Jesus said, "It is written" and "Behold I come in the volume of the book. It's written of me."

At this point, Jesus sees himself in the word of God. We're to do the same. We must walk in his footsteps.

The word of God must become our flesh.

The word is to become our flesh so it can dwell among us.

St. John 1:1 says:

"In the beginning was the Word, and the Word was with God, and the Word was God." If you are God's you should be living as a walking manifestation of His word in the earth."

When the bible was written scribes were present for a reason.

We hear a lot about affirmations and vision boards. In my book Voice-print, I share my formula for success (Vision + Voice = Velocity). There's true power in using these methodologies. Likewise, there's power in the written word of God.

It's the reason courts have transcribers and recordkeepers. It's why accountants manage books. Recordkeeping is important to God.

The children of Israel recorded every instruction, blessing, and victory. God wanted to make sure the next generation understood and heard how He'd brought them out. He said again and again, "Recite these words in their ears."

Old Testament prophets, disciples, and apostles knew the power of recordkeeping. They realized it was for history's sake. I've shared this story before. One day while traveling from Indiana down I-69, I heard God say, "The only way to right history is to write history."

At the time, I didn't understand. Then, it hit me so hard, I wrote about it in my last book. Every great president, politician, humanitarian, or world changer has written their own story. They wanted to tell sure their side of the story before history did.

Who or what will tell your story when you're gone?

Make and record history for future generations and your children's children.

This is a must for every believer. Even families who endured slavery, hardship, and separation must write their story. The nation of Israel understands this. They created an entire time of worship to remember and recite the marvelous things God did.

Israel ensures future generations are aware of all God's miraculous works and acts. They recite their time in captivity. They talk about bondage under Pharaoh's hand. They recall 40 years in the wilderness. They recount the miracle of manna. They rehearse the times' God spoke to Moses on the mountain.

How Joshua led them to the promised land is retold again and again. They share how they sent the spies to scope out the land. They remind future generations t God brought them out so they never forget.

The nation of Israel wants each generation to understand their history. With pride, they proclaim, "It is your birthright. The land belongs to you. Fight for it and hold your position!"

As a result, the Israelites still fight and hold their ground today. The blessing of Abraham and this message is for all. Anyone can grab hold. Be blessed and walk into your promised land.

Some of us are reciting things about our family, but only telling our version of the story. What has God said about you and your family? What is the entirety of the message from the beginning, middle, through the end?

Capture, recall, recount, and remember how previous generations endured and overcame. Your family's written record is a blueprint for future generations. Teach them how you triumphed and what brought you through.

Your Testimony Strengthens The Faith Of Others

If you're reading this, you've come through the fire. You've pushed and pressed to get to this moment. It's time for the world to hear your story. Shout it on the mountaintop! Someone is waiting for you.

How will a person struggling with pain pills break addiction if they don't know someone else did too? How will a promiscuous woman with low self-esteem shake free? Someone contemplating suicide needs to know there's hope to change their life around. People need an example to follow.

We're many members in one body. God shaped and formed us to need each other. I see saints and Christians acting as things that happen to others don't impact them at all. I'm tickled.

God calls us to be accountable for others and stand as watchmen on the wall. If we see something out of order, we must stop and shut it down.

"Whatever we bind on earth is bound in heaven. Whatever we loose on earth is loosed in heaven."

It's time to release your story on the earth. It's time to answer the groans and moans. The earth waits for the manifestation of the Sons of God. Will you answer the call?

We decree and believe you're answering now!

Your heavenly script must be fulfilled on earth as it is in Heaven.

You have a predestined future already appointed by God. Our lives are not our own. God has plans for each of us. So many reject the call.

My entire life I had a knowing. I knew my purpose was to share the love and word of God. Ever since I was young I was passionate about it. I received my minister's license before my second experience of church hurt. I didn't know how to move forward.

I made small efforts to move toward purpose, but something was still missing. I held back. I kept asking God, "How?" I didn't want to join another church. I knew I had a gift. I also knew gifts and callings are without repentance. You can use your gift for the wrong things, going through the motions, and still not fulfill God's plan.

I also started to resent the gift. In the past, every time I spoke up or started walking into my divine calling, something would try to shut me down. I started holding back. Over time, I became someone I didn't know. nice and congenial.

I became a people pleaser. I lost my spark. My energy went toward blending in. I gave up and stopped fighting. Many of my family and friends didn't understand my journey. I've finally accepted the call. I always answered when no one was looking.

I'd stream online to listen to Bishop Eddie Long, Dr. Bill Winston, and Pastor Jamal Bryant. I didn't want to endure the pain of rejection again.

I refused to open my heart to a group of people who may or may not accept me for who I was.

It was a deep rejection. I knew I had something to share but didn't understand how to share it, or who with. I sought affirmation in those around me. Then, I discovered affirmation and acceptance from God is all a person needs.

Now that I accepted the heavenly script, I bring who I am into everything I do. I don't have to hide my love for God. I don't have to hide my passion for His word. I don't have to shrink back. I draw the right people. They see something inside bigger, stronger, and more powerful than me. It's God.

I'm sure you can relate. God's brought me through so much. I survived a suicide attempt at 19, dated drug dealers, and was on probation. Like other 19-year-olds, I was finding my way. In His mercy, God wiped my record completely clean. He took my tears away.

I used to party, hang out, get drunk, and anything else you can imagine, but that wasn't the end of my story. Wherever you are right now in life, It's not the end of your story either. You have more to give and do. You have more to offer the world. It's time to rise. Answer the call.

Although I didn't grow up with my father, we became very close in the last 20 years of his life. We talked on the phone every day. I'd call to check on him. He'd always say, "Girl, you are a preacher. You are a preacher like me." I didn't understand it then.

I wondered how he knew since I didn't grow up with him. He didn't know my aspirations or the things hidden in my heart. After years of searching, he was affirming my identity. Now, years later after his death, I realize he saw in me what I couldn't see in myself. He was affirming for a divine purpose.

Just like God affirmed me, He is affirming you. He's healing your heart to let you know, it's alright to step out on faith. Go ahead and leap. "I got you," He says. "You're called. You're chosen for such a time as this." It's time to write your book.

IT'S TIME TO WRITE YOUR BOOK

AFTER GOD SPOKE ABOUT THE #1 thing that's wrong with the bible, he reminded me about the original men he used to write what we refer to as the "The Bible." We call this the "Word of God." It is but let's dig a little deeper.

The bible is made up of "Books of the Bible." You have Genesis, Exodus, Leviticus, Numbers, and Deuteronomy which have been called "The Pentateuch" or Books of Moses. Each book that follows is a book of someone written by a man.

King David wrote several books. Those books are associated with the revelation of God revealed throughout David's life. King Solomon wrote several books. Equally, those books correspond to the magnitude of favor and blessing bestowed on him. Each prophet has their book, the minor prophets, and major prophets alike.

In God's eyes, no voice or perspective in the Kingdom is too small. Whether we look in the old testament or new, the bible is comprised of books of the lives and testimony of great men and women who believed.

These men lived their lives as written stories being left for those that would follow. Many of our church services and sermons are based on these stories. They are still alive today.

At what point did the church stop believing that God could still speak His word through mere mortal men? God is the same yesterday, today, and forevermore. We constantly hear those who question the Bible's authenticity. Many argue books have been omitted from the bible and are missing. Why is this important?

It's important because each book, life, person, and story opens up another dimension and revelation of God's character, mind, and who He is. God never created man to live independently of others. We were created to be connected. We are one body and organism that needs each other to thrive.

We often hear many analogies used about the physical body. We hear how the head needs the toe and the toe needs the foot. Likewise, we need each other. Regardless of background, status, race, or any other thing, it's time to recognize we can't learn the entire story unless every part of the story is told.

In Isaiah, God reminds us, "His thoughts are far above our thoughts and His ways far above ours." There's a good reason. He is all-seeing, all-knowing, and all-loving. He sees and knows it all.

If we don't share our side of the story coupled with God's side too, how will others know about His goodness? How will they believe in Him? How will they know He pulled us out and through?

I write this book to the Body of Christ with urgency and conviction. God's been so good. He's pulled me out of disaster after disaster. He's taken my reckless, broken life and always putting the pieces together again. He always gently leads me safely back to Him. When I walked away, turned my back, threw my hands up and said no more, His love never failed.

It's really important to piggyback off this point to touch on one more thing. For those seasoned in the things of God who've been standing in the door blocking others from coming in, you do not escape.

You are also what's wrong with the bible.

At this moment in history, it's important everyone in the Body of Christ takes a good look at ourselves. We must assess ourselves and see ourselves through the eyes of God. This is for those who digest the parts of God's word pleasing to their ears but ignore it in its totality.

It's for those of us who embrace the riches. The ones who only embrace the blessings. Those who only embrace holiness. Yet, we don't embrace the more abase and weak things too. Galatians tells us, "Brethren if a man is overtaken in a fault, ye which are spiritual, restore such a one in the spirit of meekness; considering thyself, lest thou also be tempted."

In this text, Paul writes to those that are spiritual. He addresses those who understand what it's like to be down. Paul instructs those that know what being rejected and forgotten feels like. In a nutshell, he is saying, these are the only ones that should be opening their mouth to speak on a matter to act as the voice and heart of God.

I want to talk about this subject of rejection for a moment.

I write as an authority on this subject. The rejection I experienced was often a direct result of searching to live a life "on purpose in purpose." Most rejected me without understanding why. Rejection can be a calling.

Sometimes you have to experience deep rejection to understand the sufferings of Christ. We live in a success-driven society that wants people to believe everything is supposed to be all roses. God's formula for success is the opposite of the world's. If you pursue righteousness, you will be persecuted and lied on.

In Christ, you can love others and give your all. These same people may very well spit in your face, turn their back on you, talk bad about you, and drag your name through the mud. Most things they say won't be true and most won't care. This is a deep rejection.

I wanted to quickly touch on this because I hear many in the church praying for people who have been overtaken by a spirit of rejection. By all means, pray. However, after you are done praying, look to the scriptures as your guide. Christ was rejected. The cross was built on rejection.

Isaiah 53:3-12 KJV

He is despised and rejected of men; a man of sorrows, and acquainted with grief: and we hid as it were our faces from him; he was despised and we esteemed him not.

Surely he hath borne our griefs, and carried our sorrows: yet we did esteem him stricken, smitten of God, and afflicted.

But he was wounded for our transgressions, he was bruised for our iniquities; the chastisement of our peace was upon him; with his stripes, we are healed.

All we like sheep have gone astray; we have turned every one to his way: and the LORD hath laid on him the iniquity of us all.

He was oppressed, and he was afflicted, yet he opened not his mouth; he is brought as a lamb to the slaughter, and as a sheep, before her shearers is dumb, so he openeth not his mouth.

He was taken from prison and from judgment: and who shall declare his generation? For he was cut off out of the land of the living: for the transgression of my people was he stricken.

And he made his grave with the wicked, and with the rich in his death; because he had done no violence, neither was any deceit in his mouth.

Yet it pleased the LORD to bruise him; he hath put him to grief: when thou shalt make his soul an offering for sin, he shall see his seed, he shall prolong his days, and the pleasure of the LORD shall prosper in his hand. He shall see of the travail of his soul, and shall be satisfied: by his knowledge shall my righteous servant justify many; for he shall bear their iniquities.

Therefore will I divide him a portion with the great, and he shall divide the spoil with the strong; because he hath poured out his soul unto death: and he was numbered with the transgressors; he bore the sin of many and made intercession for the transgressors."

Christ was rejected. Yet, he was the savior of the world. Christ was in prison. Yet, he came to set the captives free. Christ was despised yet he was the Son of God, the King of Kings.

If Christ was rejected, who are we? When did we start believing that those rejected or who have grown up in circumstances less fortunate are less than? It's ridiculous. We must begin to call this thinking out. We must get our mouths off of God's people. It's time to move on to perfection and maturity.

HUMAN BEINGS FAIL TO PRACTICE
WHAT WE PREACH

AS HUMAN BEINGS, we tend to shun what we don't understand. We sometimes reject what doesn't fit in our frame of reference. All of us are guilty of this. This is another thing wrong with the bible. It's time for the Body of Christ to arise as a beacon of light. The world is looking for hope at this hour.

We can no longer fail to practice what we preach. We must show, preach, and demonstrate the entire gospel. We must also embrace the parts that don't feel good. It's time to focus on the "tiny foxes spoil the vine." We have to demonstrate the love we preach about.

I see the Body of Christ embracing some parts of itself and rejecting others. We all have a role to play in God's kingdom. Do you never know who else may be holding your deliverance in their mouth?

After being hurt in the church, I left the church building but I never left God. I still had a very deep, intimate relationship with Him. I sinned during this time. I did things I wouldn't have done had I been account-able to leadership, but that said, "My heart was always with God" hoping, believing, knowing.

I remember when I fell so deeply into a situation. I started praying and seeking God. I wanted to get back to the basics. I'd been attending a very word rich and revelatory ministry. Everything was "so deep." We were so deep that at the time we were "no earthly good." So I started crying out to God. I wanted to return to my first love.

I didn't know where to start. I finally said, "Let me just read the 10 commandments. I'm going to do my best to live by and follow them. As I studied them, "Honor the Sabbath to keep it holy," stood out. I remembered a nugget my mother shared when I was younger. It was about the Sabbath. I had never implemented it. This was after she'd had a brain aneurysm. Her voice, wisdom, and times shared became much clearer.

I decided at that moment, to honor my mother and God, my daughter and I honor the Sabbath. I heard God tell me I needed to learn how to honor the Sabbath so I could learn how to rest. At the time, I didn't know what being able to rest meant.

When I shared it with a few Christian family and friends, they laughed. They blew me off and thought something was wrong. I still did it. I tuned into Central Synagogue in New York. I sang the songs along with the congregation. I learned and read the blessings. Never once did I depart from my faith.

During this time, God taught me some of the most profound and simple lessons about His word. One day if allowed, I'll write a book and share more on insights learned. I'd like to quickly touch on one that's highly relevant to our topic about human beings as the #1 thing wrong with the bible.

The Jewish Shabbat or sabbath blessing correlates to the last supper and what the Christian church calls communion. After a few months honoring the sabbath, I realized the night Jesus took bread with his disciples before his crucifixion he was honoring the sabbath.

In the Christian church whenever communion is taken the following passage is read:

I Corinthians 11:23-32

For I have received of the Lord that which also I delivered unto you, That the Lord Jesus the same night in which he was betrayed took bread:

And when he had given thanks, he brake it, and said, Take, eat: this is my body, which is broken for you: this do in remembrance of me.

After the same manner also he took the cup, when he had supped, saying, This cup is the new testament in my blood: this do ye, as oft as ye drink it, in remembrance of me.

For as often as ye eat this bread, and drink this cup, ye do shew the Lord's death till he come.

Wherefore whosoever shall eat this bread, and drink this cup of the Lord, unworthily, shall be guilty of the body and blood of the Lord.

But let a man examine himself, and so let him eat of that bread, and drink of that cup.

For he that eateth and drinketh unworthily, eateth and drinketh damnation to himself, not discerning the Lord's body.

For this cause many are weak and sickly among you, and many sleep.

Many are weak and sick in the Body of Christ because they're not discerned.

God spoke loudly about this text. My eyes kept being led to these words, "Not discerning the Lord's body. For this cause many are weak and sickly among you, and many sleep." Revelation downloaded into my spirit.

The reason so much sickness exists in the Body of Christ is that we do not discern each other. So many of us are cursing people with our mouths and putting our tongues in other people's business where it doesn't belong. Instead of speaking life, many are speaking the very opposite. It's time to discern the Lord's body.

We must stop speaking death, cancers, and hate-filled disease. We must turn and repent. We're all one body. What you say about someone impacts, everyone. You may think you can say whatever you want about anyone. The truth is that even if that person suffers harm based on your words, the greater harm will come to you. The next verse goes on to talk about being judged.

I Corinthians 11:32 KJV

But when we are judged, we are chasted of the Lord, that we should not be condemned with the world.

God judges those who mistreat his precious sheep and misrepresent Him. Sometimes now, sometimes later. What's wrong with the Bible is that many of us are not swallowing the whole truth and nothing but the truth. We take the bits and pieces that accommodate our lifestyle or way of thinking instead of taking the whole roll. TIME OUT!

We can not truly move on to maturity, walk the walk, and be the city set on a hill if we're too busy squinting at the smallest things. It's time to stop pointing our fingers and picking out flaws. Most times these things don't even really matter to God. Do you think God cares about what Sister Sally is wearing to church?

Do you think God is shaking his head in shame because of how short her dress is? "He clothes the flowers of the field." Yes there is discretion, but how about we draw Sister Sally first. We need to draw the lost before we put our mouths on them. We can't mess up people's character and reputation with no clue what they've been through.

We, as the Body of Christ, must begin to hear those little nudges no one wants to hear. Take for example in Galatians where it talks about the works of the flesh or where it talks about backbiting, gossiping, and minding our business.

These are just a few things that we need to start putting in place to become the walking, talking, living epistles we were meant to be! There is power in becoming the word!

I'll never forget what happened last year. Something had been going on in my back for a while. Although it wasn't painful, I'd noticed it. It was just weird. I kept going and pushing through. I didn't think it was anything serious.

I'd recently quit my part-time job. I felt a strong urgency to just stop and seek the Lord. I went into deep consecration. Three weeks in, I started feeling muscle spasms in my arm. As the days went on they got tighter, longer, and stronger.

After a few days, I couldn't sleep. I couldn't lay down. I was in so much pain. I was restless no matter which way I turned or laid. I couldn't find one position to rest in. I went to urgent care.

Urgent care performed tests and prescribed pain killers. They advised me if I didn't get better in a week, I needed to go to my primary doctor. I was so medicated during that time. I literally couldn't function.

I was solely operating on Biofreeze and pain killers. Someone suggested I go to the chiropractor. I hadn't thought of that. I called around looking for a chiropractor who took my insurance. I only found one.

When I arrived for the initial consultation, surprisingly, I was greeted by worship music. The chiropractor was a Christian. He couldn't treat me at the time because he needed to analyze to get a pre-authorization. He did a quick walkthrough. Then, told me what I could purchase to help until our first visit.

Before leaving I asked if it was alright to continue the muscle relaxers and pain relievers? I'd been taking two Ibuprofen 800 a night. It was still not relieving the pain. Just thinking about it does something to me. His response was so profound. I'll never forget it.

Dr. Jeff said, "As long as you're taking the medication, your body will never produce what it needs to heal." It was a huge lightbulb moment.

I'd never looked at it that way and it was exactly what I needed. I stopped taking the medication right away. I immediately implemented his suggested interventions.

It was the absolute first time I slept in over a month. The first night I woke up 5 times repositioning myself, but by the second night, I slept through the entire night. My body was starting to heal. It felt like a miracle. No one knew what I was going through but my daughter and a few close friends.

No one checked on me to ask if I was okay. No one understood the bags under my eyes and lack of sleep. No one even cared (laugh out loud). Since that time, I have been going for regular adjustments. Dr. Jeff found two areas that need work. I was diagnosed with arthritis. A disk from my neck had been damaged.

My neck had been hung down and pushed forward for so long that it ate at the cartilage between my vertebrae. He mentioned this slight change can make someone feel like an additional 20 pounds has been added to their head.

As I started to heal and recover, I found myself praying for those in the Body of Christ in physical pain. I'd felt emotional and psychological pain, but I had never felt that kind of physical pain.

I started asking others to pray for those suffering from pain, addicted to pain medications because they couldn't find rest. Ironically, when I recovered and joined a prayer call, three other people on the call were experiencing the same thing.

It never even dawned on me before that time to pray for others dealing with physical pain. I'd never felt or seen it. If there wasn't a physical manifestation like a wheelchair or walker, I couldn't see it. I didn't know what it was to be unable to sleep at night, get rest, or even crawl out of bed because you've been up all night. I promised myself once healed, I'd never forgotten those that suffer from immense pain.

Let's explore:

1. **Although the problem started in my neck, it began to affect my back. Then it traveled to another place. The symptoms started showing up in my arm.** Many look at parts of God's body pointing the finger. They see the problem acting as if

someone doesn't matter. The onlookers don't even realize the problem didn't start there. It is the symptom, not the cause. Regardless of cause or symptom, we're connected. If issues are not dealt with they show up later and travel to other parts of the body.

2. **The damage happened over time. I didn't notice it.** I knew something was different. I knew something was going on, but I couldn't see the damage being done. I couldn't see what had been eaten away as a result.

3. **As long as I was taking pain medications my body could never produce what it needed to heal.** This happened to me for over 30 days. Can you imagine what it feels like to be living with pain for years? Can you fathom taking pain meds to heal without understanding the body has to create what it needs to heal itself? How many in the Body of Christ are hooked on spiritual narcotics keeping them from true healing?

It's a powerful revelation and concept the Body of Christ must heed and hear! We must get off the pain medication of bitterness, deception, backbiting, gossiping, whoremongering, and lying. We can no longer pretend we don't see what's happening or what's at stake. We're one Body created in Christ Jesus for His glory and His workmanship. We're many members but only one body.

Let's get off the pain medication of drunkenness and complacency. We have to heal from the inside out. We have to allow ourselves to produce to bring forth the healing we need in this hour. No medication can fix this. No numbing, mind-altering entertainment can give us what we need. It has to come from within.

1. **I needed adjustment.** The doctor couldn't tell me what was out of place in my life then I continue along as normal. This happened over time. A skillful practitioner has to manipulate and push things back in place. He adjusts what's out of alignment. I have to lie on the table, lay down my pride, and wait for the unexpected to happen.

I don't know the complete healing the next adjustment will bring. I don't know what pain will be alleviated as a result of the next push. I do know it has to be done! If I don't show up for the appointments or take the doctor's advice, I'll stay in the same condition. If I don't go, I'll stay out of alignment bent in the same position.

It's time for the Body of Christ to adjust and align with the plans and purposes of God on earth as it is in Heaven. We need the members and bones pushed back together in their rightful place. We must make room for the cartilage to grow back to hold us together.

Success can no longer mean us and our families making it alone. Our success is dependent on the success of God's kingdom and His Body. We can't blame the devil for anything and everything. Which brings me to another thing wrong with the bible.

WE, GIVE THE DEVIL TOO MUCH PRESS

I CAN'T HEAR certain messages anymore. I get frustrated when I log in to get a word to feed my soul or show up to hear a preacher preach, only to be bombarded with what the devil is doing. I think to myself, "I can't wait until I can finally deliver this message to the church." STOP giving the enemy so much press.

I do get it. In the black church, there was a time we weren't allowed to speak about what was happening openly and publicly. Our enslaved ancestors risked being beaten or killed if they spoke against their masters. I believe this is where this may have started. I could be wrong, but this is my personal opinion.

When bad things happened, we couldn't say Mr. or Mrs. So and So did this or that. However, over time this developed into a dangerous trend. We became the enemy's publicist and focused more on what he was doing instead of God. This deception needs to be broken.

Before you pick up stones to stone me, let me explain. I know there is a very real adversary at work. The bible tells us:

Ephesians 6:12 KJV

"We wrestle not against flesh and blood, but against principalities, against powers, against the rulers of the darkness of this world, against spiritual wickedness in high places."

We as believers are not wrestling against people. We're wrestling against systems, ideologies, and ancient forces that have been established for years attempting to block the plan and purposes of the Living God.

Why? Why are these forces blinding the minds of the masses? Why do these forces care about your freedom and liberty here on earth? Because the truth makes you free. It makes you free from the burden and worry of debt. It makes you free from mental chains, bondage, and slavery.

When you stop caring about the material, temporary things you become a threat to the status quo. We live in a world full of control. It's about being controlled by someone else's agenda.

What can God do with a life fully submitted and surrendered? What can God do with a life that sells out dying to themselves? Ask Jesus. He rose with all power in HIs hand!

Colossians 2:8-17 KJV

8 Beware lest any man spoil you through philosophy and vain deceit, after the tradition of men, after the rudiments of the world, and not after Christ.

9 For in him dwelleth all the fulness of the Godhead bodily.

10 And ye are complete in him, which is the head of all principality and power:

11 In whom also ye are circumcised with the circumcision made without hands, in putting off the body of the sins of the flesh by the circumcision of Christ:

12 Buried with him in baptism, wherein also ye are risen with him through the faith of the operation of God, who hath raised him from the dead.

13 And you, being dead in your sins and the uncircumcision of your flesh, hath he quickened together with him, having forgiven you all trespasses;

14 Blotting out the handwriting of ordinances that was against us, which was contrary to us, and took it out of the way, nailing it to his cross;

15 And having spoiled principalities and powers, he made a shew of them openly, triumphing over them in it.

16 Let no man therefore judge you in meat, or in drink, or in respect of an holyday, or of the new moon, or of the sabbath days:

17 Which are a shadow of things to come; but the body is of Christ.

In this text we see:

1. Christ is the head of all principality and power.
2. In him dwelleth all the fullness of the Godhead bodily.
3. We are complete "in him."
4. He was raised and we rise with him.
5. All ordinances against us have been forgiven and blotted out. They have been nailed to the cross.
6. Christ spoiled principalities and powers making an open show of them. In the Greek text, spoil means to "plunder, loot, or something taken from another by force or craft. It applies to what belongs by right or custom to the victor in war or political contest (merriam-webster.com). Not only did God spoil the principalities, but it was also a beautiful spectacle at the same time. He made an open shew of them. He did it in public, for all to see!
7. Because of the death, burial, and resurrection of the Lord Jesus Christ no man can judge you in anything but the Living God! No one. He abolished the judgment. He withdrew the verdict.

He took every lie, accusation, and curse and blotted them out and away. Your record in Heaven is completely clean.

After taking away our sin, degradation, death, and shame, Christ goes a step further. He says now, "In me, you are eternally blessed. In me, you are eternally free. In me, you have joy unspeakable, life abundantly, righteousness, and full vindication. Have you ever seen your enemies receive vindication? It's a dangerous thing!

Let's stop giving the enemy free press! We must begin to lift our King and tell a dying world why He alone is the risen savior. The devil is the father of lies and the master of deception. He's so skillful he has the world believing he's bigger than he is. This is how revelation describes him:

Revelation 17:7-11

And the angel said unto me, Wherefore didst thou marvel? I will tell thee the mystery of the woman, and of the beast that carrieth her, which hath the seven heads and ten horns.

The beast that thou sawest was, and is not; and shall ascend out of the bottomless pit, and go into perdition: and they that dwell on the earth shall wonder, whose names were not written in the book of life from the foundation of the world, whey they behold the beast that was and is not, and yet is.

And here is the mind which hath wisdom. The seven heads are seven mountains, on which the woman sitteth.

And there are seven kings: five are fallen, and one is, and the other is not yet come; and when he cometh, he must continue a short space.

And the beast that was, and is not, even he is the eighth and is of the seven, and goeth into perdition.

So, the question is, what are you waiting on? The devil doesn't have the power to stop you. Only you have that power. Stop giving him so much press!

Maybe you're like I was. You've been through so much hell, you forgot there's a day of resurrection. Maybe you forgot God is waiting on you to ascend to your throne to be seated in Him right where He is. Maybe you forgot what he endured on your behalf.

Do you realize he put the devil eternally under your feet right where He lives and belongs? Do you know the only chance he has to tell his side of the story is if you allow it? Step up to the plate to walk in your divine destiny, true calling, and purpose?

THE WORLD IS WAITING ON YOU

THIS BOOK IS for those with a deep love for God. It is for the broken, wounded, rejected, and those who have been left to die. You maybe like the "certain man" found in Luke chapter 10 who went down to Jericho who fell among thieves. He was stripped of his raiment and wounded. The thieves departed leaving him dead.

Do you feel counted out? Do you feel as though you've been left for dead? Have you' seemingly been robbed of your innocence or dreams? Maybe you've been through so much chaos in life, you feel you can't find God again. Regardless of why you're in this place on the side of the road, God chose you to accomplish His will.

The fact you're reading this means you're divinely positioned for an adjustment, quickening, and set up. It's time for you to become God's living word in the earth. Maybe you served in ministry and something devastating happened. Maybe it knocked the very wind out of you. Did it make you turn your heart against God's people?

At one time that was me. I felt used. I felt those in leadership over-looked the very ones that secretly carried them through. I carried the burden of those praying for others often being mismanaged. Bitterness had crept in my heart. I didn't realize at the time it was eating me alive. I didn't care that we are all connected. I didn't understand why there appeared to be "big I's" and "little you's" in the Kingdom of God.

I Corinthians 12:3-31 KJV

3 Wherefore I give you to understand, that no man speaking by the Spirit of God calleth Jesus accursed: and that no man can say that Jesus is the Lord but by the Holy Ghost.

4 Now there are diversities of gifts, but the same Spirit.

5 And there are differences of administrations, but the same Lord.

6 And there are diversities of operations, but it is the same God which worketh all in all.

7 But the manifestation of the Spirit is given to every man to profit withal.

8 For to one is given by the Spirit the word of wisdom; to another the word of knowledge by the same Spirit;

9 To another faith by the same Spirit; to another the gifts of healing by the same Spirit;

10 To another the working of miracles; to another prophecy; to another discerning of spirits; to another divers kinds of tongues; to another the interpretation of tongues:

11 But all these worketh that one and the selfsame Spirit, dividing to every man severally as he will.

12 For as the body is one, and hath many members, and all the members of that one body, being many, are one body: so also is Christ.

13 For by one Spirit are we all baptized into one body, whether we be Jews or Gentiles, whether we be bond or free; and have been all made to drink into one Spirit.

14 For the body is not one member, but many.

15 If the foot shall say, Because I am not the hand, I am not of the body; is it therefore not of the body?

16 And if the ear shall say, Because I am not the eye, I am not of the body; is it therefore not of the body?

17 If the whole body

18 But now hath God set the members every one of them in the body, as it hath pleased him.

19 And if they were all one member, where were the body?

20 But now are they many members, yet but one body.

21 And the eye cannot say unto the hand, I have no need of thee: nor again the head to the feet, I have no need of you.

This passage is a reminder that God cares about people.

He cares about the details. If He didn't the text wouldn't go to such lengths to spell out His expectations. I'm not sure where the hierarchical thinking snuck in.

Some believe sitting in a pulpit automatically qualifies someone to deserve more honor than the usher greeting at the door. As a black mother, I teach my daughter the principle of proper honor all the time. It is easy to get caught up in big versus little, good versus bad, or black versus white. The only thing you should judge or know a tree by is the fruit it bears. Pure and simple.

I want my daughter to know what I wish someone taught me at a very young age. You can watch what someone does and listen to what they say to know who they are. It's not rocket science. It shouldn't matter who a person is or what position they hold, what is their fruit?

Is it saltwater or fresh? The bible says they can't both come out of the same mouth or place. Blessing and cursing can't come out at the same time. I'm amazed when leaders become so defensive when someone says something they don't want to hear.

I agree blatant disrespect mixed with the wrong intention shouldn't be embraced. Yet, if someone comes in meekness" to address and correct a situation, why block what's said?

There's no place for politics in the church. Sometimes based on our position or perspectives we choose sides. Then, out of emotion or anger, we start saying things. The fear of God should restrain us from saying just anything about God's people.

There is too much divisiveness and discord in the Body of Christ. Yet, we walk in church Sunday after Sunday, lift our hands in praise, and ignore the hurt we've caused someone else. God is not coming back for a fragmented body. He will only return for the bride. I've never understood it. It's not biblical. It's what's wrong with the bible. We must start to reflect on what we've read.

I John 4:6-12 KJV

We are of God: he that knoweth God heareth us; he that is not of God heareth not us. Hereby know we the spirit of truth, and the spirit of error.

Beloved, let us love one another: for love is of God; and every one that loveth is born of God, and knoweth God.

He that loveth not knoweth not God; for God is love.

In this was manifested the love of God toward us, because that God sent his only begotten Son into the world, that we might live through him.

Herein is love, not that we loved God, but that he loved us, and sent his Son to be the propitiation for our sins.

Beloved, if God so loved us, we ought also to love one another.

No man hath seen God at any time. If we love one another, God dwelleth in us, and his love is perfected in us.

I am sharing this passage because it's critical we shake religion, grab hold of Christ, take up our crosses, and follow Him every day!

I observe people. I see a lot and sometimes never say a word. Some are fooled by my demeanor. I can come across as very congenial. Sometimes I am. Other times, I'm smiling to keep from cringing on the inside every time.

During some of my hard times, I'd hear those claiming to be saints whispering against me. I'd see people coming from a mile away that meant me no good at all. With love and grace, I'd attempt to show God's love the best way I knew how.

I've found that sometimes people need to be confronted and checked. You have to let them know, "I see you." I see a lot of people who claim they love God but don't love people. How is that possible? There's no way. The fruit isn't there.

When you truly love somebody and have a disagreement you come together to hash it out. I've seen too many people quickly dismiss others as irrelevant to their spiritual journey. Then I realize although they have a title and position, they are still spiritually immature.

Let me back this up with scripture:

St. Matthew 5:20-24 KJV

For I say unto you, That except your righteousness shall exceed the righteousness of the scribes and Pharisees, ye shall in no case enter into the kingdom of heaven.

Ye have heard that it was said of them of old time, Thou shalt not kill; and whosoever shall kill shall be in danger of the judgment:

But I say unto you, That whosoever is angry with his brother without a cause shall be in danger of the judgment: and whosoever shall say to his brother, Raca, shall be in danger of the council: but whosoever shall say, Thou fool, shall be in danger of hell fire.

Therefore if thou bring thy gift to the altar, and there rememberest that they brother hath ought against thee;

Leave there thy gift before the altar, and go thy way: first be reconciled to thy brother, and then come and offer thy gift."

Many believers today are not walking in their calling because of a petty disagreement. God didn't intend for it to be this way. We come from different walks of lives and perspectives, but should still be unified as one body towards a common goal.

The Lord never intended for denominations to disrupt the flow in the Body of Christ. When Christ walked the earth, his humility was so amazing, he said, "Don't even worship me." He commanded those who worshipped him, to worship God!

Revelation 19:10 KJV

"And I fell at his feet to worship him. And he said unto me, See thou do it not: I am thy fellow-servant, and of thy brethren that have the testimony of Jesus: worship God: for the testimony of Jesus is the spirit of prophecy."

Jesus made it clear, we are joint-heirs with him. That's why it's imperative we get it right so we don't misrepresent him to the world. We are not a church that is divided and scattered church without direction. We're not confused or fragmented. His body was broken for us. A unified body was so important to Christ this is one of the last prayers he prayed:

St. John 17 KJV

These words spake Jesus, and lifted his eyes to heaven, and said, Father, the hour is come; glorify thy Son, that they Son also may glorify thee:

As thou has given him power over all flesh, that he should give eternal life to as many as thou has given him.

And this is life eternal, that they might know thee the only true God, and Jesus Christ, whom thou hast sent.

I have glorified thee on the earth: I have finished the work which thou gavest me to do.

And now, O Father, glorify thou me with thine own self with the glory which I had with thee before the world was.

I have manifested thy name unto them which thou gavest me out of the world: thine they were, and thou gavest them me: and they have kept thy word.

Now they have known that all things whatsoever thou hast given me are of thee.

For I have given unto them the words which thou gavest me; and they have received them, and have known surely that I came out from thee, and they have believed that thou didst send me.

I pray for them: I pray not for the world, but for them which thou has given me: for they are thine.

And all mine are thine, and thine are mine; and I am glorified in them.

And now I am no more in the world, but these are in the world, and I come to thee. Holy Father, keep through thine own name those whom thou has given me, that they may be one, as we are.

While I was with them in the world, I kept them in thy name: those that thou gavest me I have kept, and none of them is lost, but the son of perdition; that the scripture might be fulfilled.

And now come I to thee; and these things I speak in the world, that they might have my joy fulfilled in themselves.

I have given them thy word; and the world hath hated them, because they are not of the world, even as I am not of the world.

I pray not that thou shouldest take them out of this world, but that thou shouldest keep them from the evil.

They are not of the world, even as I am not of the world.

Sanctify them through thy truth: thy word is truth.

As thou hast sent me into the world, even so have I also sent them into the world.

And for their sakes I sanctify myself, that they also might be sanctified through the truth.

Neither pray I for these alone, but for them also which shall believe on me through their word;

That they all may be one; as thou, father, art in me, and I in thee, that they also may be one in us: that the world may believe that thou hast sent me.

And the glory which thou gavest me I have given them; that they may be one, even as we are one:

I in them, and thou in me, that they may be made perfect in one; and that the world may know that thou hast sent me, and hast loved them, as thou hast loved me.

Father, I will that they also, whom thou hast given me, be with me where I am; that they may behold my glory, which thou hast given me: for thou lovedst me before the foundation of the world.

O righteous Father, the world hath not known thee: but I have known thee, and these have known that thou hast sent me.

And I have declared unto them thy name, and will declare it: that the love wherewith thou hast loved me may be in them, and I in them."

IT'S TIME TO MAKE THINGS RIGHT

WE'RE COMMANDED to love one another. It's time to stop defending our isms and schisms. In this political and religious climate, we must be especially careful to guard our words and make sure they align with Heaven. If our behaviors and activities don't align, this is the season to get it right.

We need you and your story. We need your power and testimony. We need your insight into the divine character and presence of God. Without it, the scriptures can't continue to "become flesh."

It's time to rise to fulfill God's call. Whether you've been in church for years, are struggling with your faith, or a new believer starting, your voice and experience matter to God. They matter to others just like me.

Regardless of if you're inside the church doors or without, we all play a role in ensuring that the bible gets it right every time! If we have faith the size of a mustard seed, we can say to this mountain, "Be removed and get out of our way."

So I say to the mountain to your destiny, **"Move! Get out of the way. Be cast into the sea!**

I say to the doubters, those who have hurt you and rejected you, **"Move! Get out of the way. Be cast into the sea!**

I say to every circumstance and opposition showing up in your life to **"Be removed now in Jesus' name!**

I'd like to end with prayer. If you've experienced rejection, stagnation, and confusion about your purpose or have walked away from God because of some deep hurt, repeat after me:

Heavenly Father, thank you that I'm what you got right with the bible. When the enemy said I was wrong, you called me righteous. You called me right.

Father, thank you for accepting me just as I am. Thank you that I don't have to jump through hoops to receive your salvation, blessing, and redemption. I can just choose to freely open my heart.

Thank you for helping me fulfill your plan and purposes for my life on the earth. Thank you for creating me in your image. Thank you for renewing the spirit of my mind, delivering me from all affliction, divinely protecting me and making me yours.

Father, thank you for your promise that when I am in your hand, **no man can pluck me out**! I praise you for my rightful seat in your Kingdom. Thank you that there is room for me at the table.

Father, I thank you that you also prepare a table before me in the presence of my enemies. Thank you for not only making me in your image but also allowing me to see your reflection every time. I am grateful when I look in the mirror I see and hear your voice every time.

Lord, you are the creator of every good and perfect gift and when you created me, you said, "It is good. I call myself what you do and completely yield to your power, purpose, salvation, and plan. Amen.

Grace and peace be unto you. May you prosper in all you do!

AUTHOR'S NOTES

EVERY YEAR I have the privilege to speak to new audiences around the world to ignite hope and transformation. There is nothing more satisfying than seeing new relationships form, dead dreams come alive, and untapped potential turn to power.

I remember the first time I spoke in front of an audience. I was a 14-year-old Texan with a message for the world. I was born to speak and teach. I love connecting with audiences to share real-world experiences, proven principles, and breakthrough strategies.

I've spent decades inspiring and investing in people. I've challenged the status quo and provoked change with powerful messages that go against conventional wisdom. Whether a Fortune 500 company, educational institution, or nonprofit, my passion is to help others break out-of-the-box to see new possibilities and experience exponential growth.

Thank you for reading this book! When I wrote the book I was in a time of deep reflection. At that time, I realized I was looking in others for what I'd hope to find within. I pray you are inspired to take action and run quickly into the open arms of your Heavenly Father. He's always there to pick us up when we need Him most.

WHO IS LONNA HARDIN

Lonna's musical career began at the early age of 5. At 12, she found herself in the spotlight when she recorded with gospel music legend, Charles Fold. By the age of 16, a nickname emerged, "Songbird."

Now, Lonna sings, writes, and speaks, with audiences around the world. She's also a voice to add light to issues that impact the voiceless and vulnerable.

In 2006, Lonna made her first solo debut as a featured artist on the "New Soul," with radio hits, "I Belong To You," "Tender Mercy," "Can't Nobody," and "Everything."

Lonna's smooth, sultry voice has been featured on the top 150 U.S. gospel stations and around the world. She also received worldwide recognition as #17 on the International Top 30 Artist list.

Lonna has shared the stage with General Colin Powell, Dorinda Clark-Cole, Marvin Sapp, Ben Tankard, Lisa Page Brooks, and more. She has worked with well-known producers including Chip Dixson, Berris Bolton, and Executive Producer Roger Ryan of Aftertouch Music.

Lonna is acclaimed author of several books including, "Voiceprint and the Melody's Song children's book series, as well as a powerful faith-based series. Her books are featured at libraries, bookstores, museums, and and events across the country.

You've seen or heard her inspire on TBN, Black Gospel, Storytelling Companion, and television or radio stations around the world.

Lonna Hardin's high-spirited energy and message of hope is why audiences say they experience the "wow factor' after hearing Lonna sing or speak at conferences, workshops, seminars, and events.

Lonna Hardin Enterprises
lonnahardin.com

www.ingramcontent.com/pod-product-compliance
Lightning Source LLC
Chambersburg PA
CBHW030814090426
42737CB00010B/1270